EVALUATING YOUR HOME

No one would leave a window open all winter. But tote up all your home's leaks and areas lacking insulation, and you may find you've as good as done so. With a typical household spending 46% of its energy budget on heating and cooling (see the chart on p. 3), those little problems can add up to a big expense.

Fortunately, most energy-saving improvements are easy to do. A missing door sweep, a clogged furnace filter, and dusty refrigerator coils can be dealt with quickly. Even bringing your attic insulation up to par can be done in a weekend. Tackling these simple chores can lower your energy bills by 5% to 30%, according to the Department of Energy (DOE). With annual household energy costs averaging $2,200 a year, that can save you a lot of money.

So grab a flashlight and a tape measure and use the Energy Savings Checklist at the back of this booklet to evaluate your house.

TISSUE PAPER TEST. To check for leaky spots, do the tissue paper test. Hold a long strip of bathroom tissue along the edge of window sashes or doors. Watch for movement.

QUICK TIP Spiders build webs where insects get into the house, a sign that a nearby window may be gappy.

WHAT YOU'LL NEED

Shown here are the basic DIY tools for common home energy projects.
Additional tools and materials are listed with each individual project.

Tape measure

Tin snips

Utility knife

Square

Miter box

Hammer

Nail sets

Light-duty staple gun

T-bevel

Self-centering nail set

Heavy-duty staple gun

Electric stapler/ brad nailer

Spring clamps

Reversible flush-cut saw

Hacksaw

Mini hacksaw

Double-edge pull saw

Folding sawhorse

USING ENERGY WISELY

It's no secret that the largest proportion of home energy goes toward heating and cooling. But a glance at the chart below shows that things like water heating, appliances, and lighting also stack up as high priorities. Changing habits and making a few easy upgrades will help you use energy wisely—and spare the household budget.

HOUSEHOLD ENERGY USE*	PERCENTAGE OF TOTAL HOUSEHOLD ENERGY USE	PORTION OF $2,200 TYPICAL HOME ENERGY EXPENDITURE
Heating	29%	$638
Cooling	17%	$374
Water heating	14%	$308
Appliances (refrigerator, dishwasher, washer, and dryer)	13%	$286
Lighting	12%	$264
Electronics (computer, monitor, TV, DVD player)	4%	$88
Other (stoves, ovens, small appliances, telephones, built-in fans)	11%	$242

*Source: Lawrence Berkeley National Laboratory, 2009

WEATHERSTRIP WINDOWS

Windows have a tough job. They have to seal out winter gusts, yet open easily when spring breezes arrive. Any place where a sash slides or a casement opens is prone to infiltration. And, of course, if your window has rattling panes or missing glazing, it is bound to leak. For the quickest results when adding weatherstripping, start with your worst cases on the windward side of your house.

WHERE WINDOWS LEAK

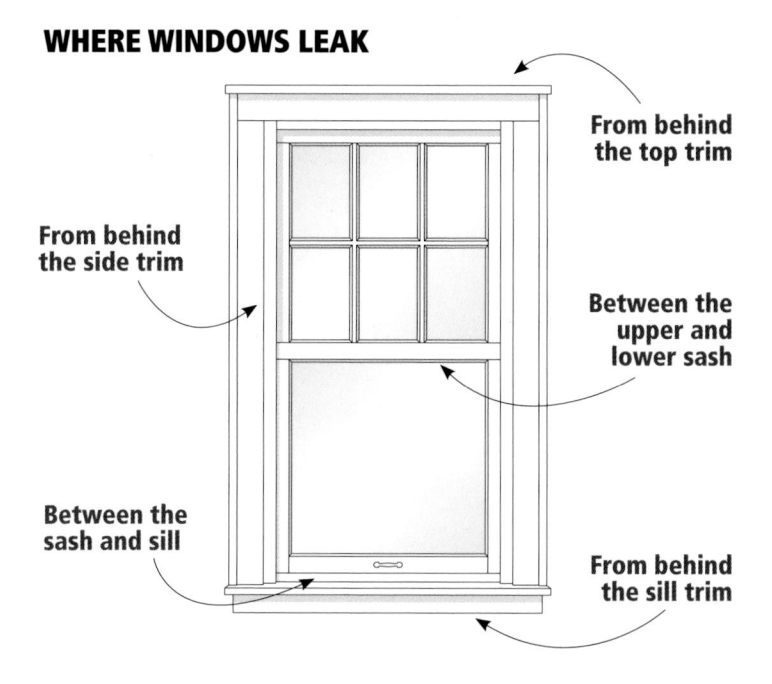

From behind the top trim

From behind the side trim

Between the upper and lower sash

Between the sash and sill

From behind the sill trim

Rope Caulk, Simple and Seasonal

It ain't pretty, but rope caulk goes on quickly to effectively seal out drafts. The downside is you'll have to remove it in the spring to open windows and reapply it in the fall when you button things up.

INSTALLING PLASTIC V-STRIP WEATHERSTRIPPING

V-strip weatherstripping installs quickly. Its springiness fills the gap between the sash and the jamb, providing an effective weather seal. It's not the prettiest or longest-lasting stuff in the world, but it's a great solution for out-of-the-way windows like basement awning windows (shown). Before installing, open the window and thoroughly clean the jamb.

What You'll Need: Self-adhesive V-strip; rag and cleaner; scissors

1. CUT A STRIP. Instead of measuring, hold the strip where you want to apply it and mark. Cut and test the fit.

2. FOLD THE STRIP. With the adhesive tape outward, run the V-strip between your thumb and forefinger so it folds on itself.

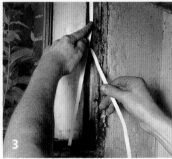

3. ADHERE THE STRIP TO THE JAMB. With the opening of the V facing outdoors, stick the strip to the jamb, removing the paper backing as you go.

INSTALLING SPRING BRONZE WEATHERSTRIPPING

Bronze weatherstripping is a tried-and-true solution that will last the life of window. It works best for small, consistent gaps. Be careful not to crimp the strip as you work, and watch for sharp edges as you cut.

What You'll Need: Spring bronze weatherstripping and brads (they are usually sold together); tape measure; tin snips; hammer; nail set; utility knife

1. MARK THE TOP OF THE SASH.
Shut the window and make a mark at the top edge of the sash.

2. ROUGH-CUT THE SPRING BRONZE.
Raise the window sash. Use a tin snips to cut one end of the strip to match the sill angle.

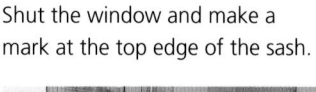

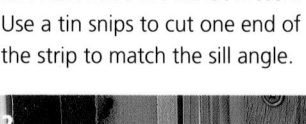

3. SLIP THE STRIP IN PLACE.
Square-cut the strip about 2 in. longer than the height of the sash. Slip it between the open sash and the jamb.

4. PREDRILL FOR THE BRADS.

Tape the strip to hold it in place. Beginning at the sill, drill ¹⁄₁₆-in. pilot holes for the brads—they're hard to start otherwise. Work your way up, keeping the strip taut.

5. FASTEN THE TOP OF THE STRIP.

Close the sash and secure the top of the strip with two brads.

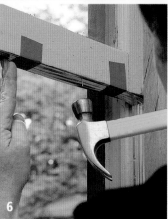

QUICK TIP To increase the spring in the strip, run the tip of a putty knife along the bend nearest the nails. Repeat until the bronze makes firm contact with the sash.

6. ATTACH SPRING BRONZE TO THE SASH BOTTOM.
Cut a piece of spring bronze to size, and tape it to the underside of the sash. Orient it so it springs open outward, and nail it in place.

ADDING SELF-STICK FOAM

Ideal for casement or awning windows or anywhere you find large, uneven gaps, self-stick foam is inexpensive and installs quickly. It won't last more than a few seasons but is well worth the trouble of occasional replacement.

What You'll Need: Self-stick foam; rag and cleaner; scissors

1. PEEL OFF THE BACKING AND APPLY. Cut a strip of self-stick foam slightly longer than you need. Peel and adhere one end, then work your way along, peeling and sticking as you go.

2. TRIM THE FOAM. Before peeling and sticking the last bit, trim it with scissors to the length needed.

INSTALLING INSULATING FILM

Shrink wrapping a leaky window or patio door is a quick way to brace for winter. The plastic film seals out drafts and captures an insulating layer of air. Come springtime, you simply strip away the film. The tape releases with the help of a hair dryer.

What You'll Need: Insulating film kit; scissors; hair dryer; utility knife

1. APPLY THE TAPE. Apply the double-sided tape, peeling off one protective strip as you adhere the tape. Cut the tape a little long; trim it to size as you finish.

2. APPLY THE FILM. Remove the outer strip from the tape. Cut an overlarge piece of film. Starting at the top, lightly press the edges of the film to the tape. If it's out of kilter, pull off the film and start again.

3. HEAT-SHRINK AND TRIM. Run your finger along the edges to firmly stick the film to the tape. Beginning in an upper corner, shrink the film using a hair dryer, keeping it a couple of inches from the surface. Trim the excess film with a utility knife.

WEATHERSTRIPPING A DOOR

It's always wise to add a storm door to provide added protection in the winter and, with the addition of a screen, cool breezes in the summer. Even with such defense, a door can leak. Well-insulated steel or fiberglass doors offer added protection over traditional wood doors, but they may leak around the perimeter. Adding spring bronze (see p. 11) or tubular gasket (see p. 13) keeps out the drafts. A sweep or shoe (see p. 14) puts the kibosh on leaks underneath the door.

WHERE DOORS LEAK

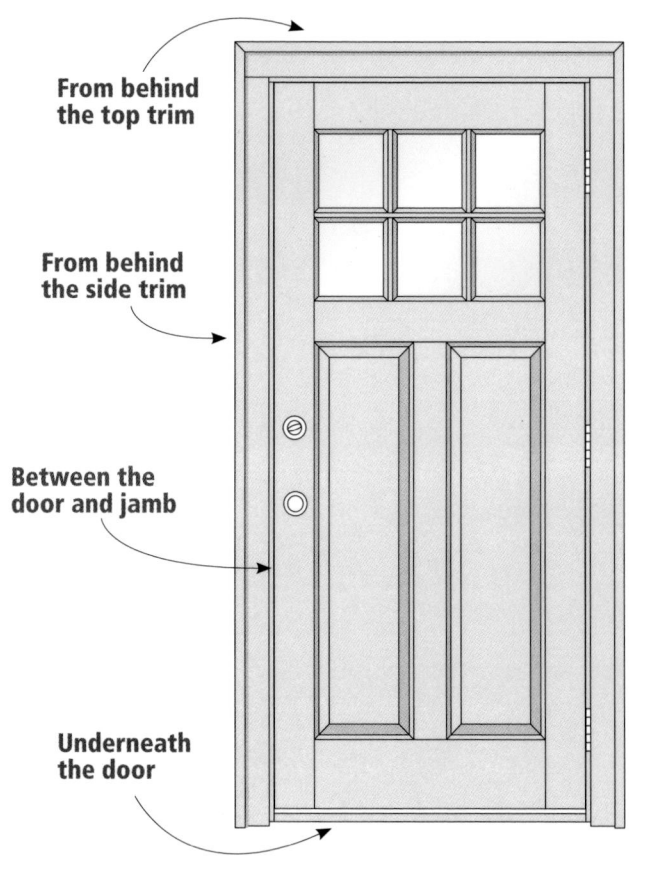

From behind the top trim

From behind the side trim

Between the door and jamb

Underneath the door

ADDING SPRING BRONZE WEATHERSTRIPPING

Spring bronze is an attractive and long-lasting way to seal doors. The only challenge is cutting out for the strike. On the hinge jamb, the bronze should spring open toward the hinge pins. On the strike side, apply it so it opens toward the stop trim.

What You'll Need: Spring bronze and brads; tape measure; tin snips; utility knife; drill/driver; hammer; nail set

1. TAPE THE STRIP IN PLACE. True to its name, spring bronze wants to spring back into a coil. To make your job easier, cut the strip a bit long and tape it into position. For the best seal, orient the hinge strip so it opens toward the inside as shown.

2. SET THE NAILS. The jamb trim can make it hard to nail without doing damage. Drill a shallow pilot hole to make it easy to start each nail. Use a 1/8-in. nail set to drive the nails home.

5. NAIL AROUND THE STRIKE PLATE.
So the strip won't catch on the door, nail around the strike plate. Apply a strip to the top jamb, orienting it the same way.

4. CUT OUT FOR THE STRIKE PLATE.
On the latch side of the jamb, place the strip so it opens away from the door. Mark and cut out for the strike plate with tin snips. Use several swipes with a utility knife to make the final vertical cut.

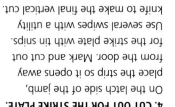

3. WORK YOUR WAY DOWN. Spring bronze can buckle, so work your way down the strip hole by hole. About a foot from the bottom of the door, use a tin snips to trim the bronze for a precise fit.

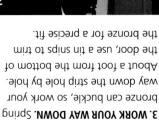

INSTALLING TUBULAR GASKET WEATHERSTRIP

Applied to the outside of a door, a wood stop equipped with tubular gasket weatherstripping flexes to make a tight seal. Newer doors have such a strip built-in. The strip wears out with time—not to mention the abuse it takes from your cat. Home centers carry generic replacements that snap into place.

What You'll Need: Weatherstrip; 4d finishing nails; tape measure; miter box and saw; utility knife; hammer; nail set

1. COPE A MITER FOR A NEAT JOINT. Starting with the top of the jamb, measure and square-cut the strip using a fine-toothed saw and a miter box. Use a tin snips to cut the tubular gasket. Before cutting the side pieces to length, remove the gasket and cut the stop at a 45-degree angle. Cope out the excess.

2. CHECK THE FIT. Hold the piece in place and check the fit. Trim as necessary using a utility knife. When satisfied with the fit, trim to exact length.

3. DRILL PILOT HOLES AND FASTEN. To avoid splitting the stop, drill a pilot hole for each 4d finishing nail. Pound the nail almost home, then drive it slightly beneath the surface of the wood with a nail set. Putty and, with the gasket removed, paint.

QUICK TIP Snip the gasket at a miterlike angle in each corner for a neat fit.

ADDING A DOOR SWEEP

A rubber or brush-type door sweep seals out cold air without impairing the way your door closes. Choose a type that attaches with screws—peel-and-stick sweeps seldom withstand use, especially on a painted door.

What You'll Need: Sweep; miter box; hacksaw; drill/driver and bit; tape

1. MARK AND CUT THE SWEEP. Open the door. Hold the sweep along the bottom of the door, and mark. For a neat, straight cut, use a hacksaw and miter box. Shut the door, and tape the sweep in place so it firmly contacts the threshold.

2. INSTALL TWO SCREWS AND TEST. At each end, drill pilot holes in the middle of the elongated hole to allow for adjustment. Install two screws and test. Adjust as needed, and add the rest of the screws.

QUICK TIP A door shoe, an alternative type of sweep, caps the bottom of your door and incorporates a gasket—sometimes an exterior drip cap as well.

SEALING GAPS AND LEAKS

Older homes are notoriously leaky, but even new homes have spots that need sealing. In fact, any opening made in your home's fabric introduces energy-sapping separations. An added benefit of sealing gaps: You'll put the lid on places insects and rodents can get into your house. Caulk can handle any gap ¼ in. or less. See p. 17 for handling larger gaps.

What You'll Need: Caulk; no-drip caulk gun

1. APPLY THE CAULK. Trim the nozzle square, leaving a ⅛-in. hole. Holding the gun at a 45-degree angle to the wall, apply the caulk with a smooth, continuous motion.

2. SMOOTH THE BEAD. Run your finger along the bead to remove excess caulk, and smooth the bead.

> **QUICK TIP** Seal now with 100% silicone clear, paintable caulk and touch up later. The clear caulk looks fine until you can get around to painting.

INSULATING RECEPTACLE AND SWITCH BOXES

In most walls, there is only 3½ in. between the drywall and the exterior sheathing. An electrical box is almost as deep, creating an uninsulated void covered only by the switch or receptacle cover. Adding a foam insert insulates and seals the opening.

What You'll Need: Receptacle/switch insulation; voltage tester; screwdriver

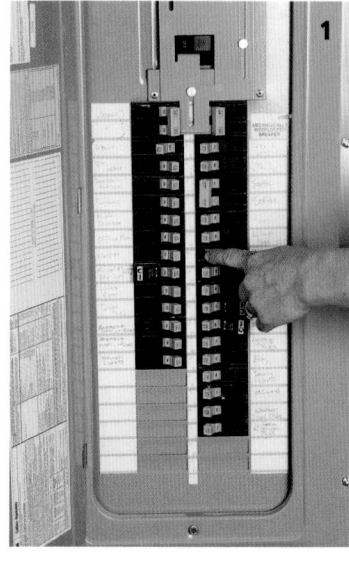

1. TURN OFF THE POWER. Remove the danger of a shock by switching off the power at your electrical panel. Remove the receptacle cover, and test to confirm that the power is off. (Even with this safeguard, handle the device as if power is ON.)

2. PUSH ON THE INSULATION. Punch out the waste pieces as necessary, and push the foam sealer onto the device. Replace the cover, and switch on the power.

QUICK TIP For added protection, seal the gap between the box and the surrounding drywall with caulk.

SEALING AROUND PIPES AND DUCTS

Energy-stealing voids can show up any place a pipe, dryer duct, or communication cable enters an exterior wall. They also appear along the foundation sill where wood might rot or masonry degrade. Spray-foam sealant is a great way to seal and insulate. Check the label when buying your sealant. Some types expand—a good idea for a large void in a wall but not so good where it might cause a window or door jamb to bulge. Some types stay spongy, while others harden for easy trimming and smoothing.

What You'll Need: Spray-foam sealant; utility knife

SEALING A GAP. Fill only half the void as you work around the gap—even minimally expanding foam blooms outward. After it dries, trim away excess with a utility knife.

QUICK TIP Wear gloves and old clothing when working with spray foam—the stuff sticks like crazy. And be sure to wear safety glasses.

QUICK TIP Check for gaps outdoors as well. Where there is a sloppy opening indoors, there may be one outside as well.

REGLAZING A WINDOW

If a wintry blast rattles your windows, chances are good you have panes with played-out glazing. Glazing is a beveled bead of putty that, with some bits of metal called "points," holds glass in the window sash. If you have old-fashioned wood storm windows, they'll most likely need reglazing, too. For the quickest benefit, start with the windows on the windward side of house.

What You'll Need: Putty; points; chisel; putty knife; brush

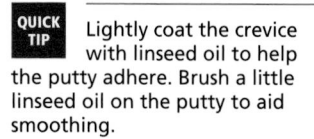 **QUICK TIP** Lightly coat the crevice with linseed oil to help the putty adhere. Brush a little linseed oil on the putty to aid smoothing.

2. APPLY AND SMOOTH THE NEW PUTTY. Rub the putty between your palms to make a long snake. Push it into the joint along the glass and the frame. Use a putty knife held at a 45-degree angle to remove excess putty. With repeated strokes, smooth the putty. After a few days, prime and paint.

1. CLEAN OUT THE OLD PUTTY.
Using a chisel and a putty knife, pry out loose putty. Push in new points with your putty knife. Brush out any loose debris.

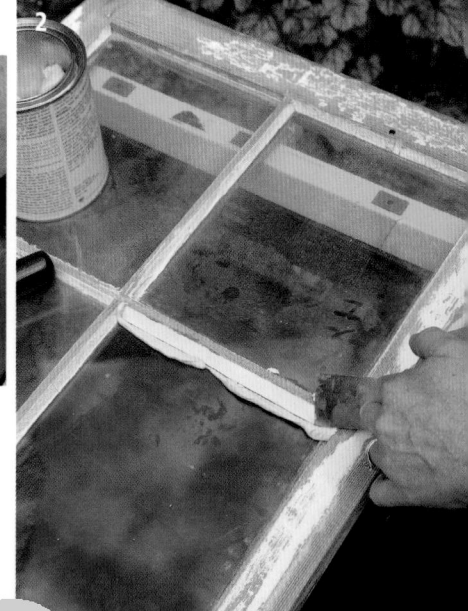

 QUICK TIP Use a heat gun to soften stubborn putty.

ADDING ATTIC INSULATON

If you want to know where to insulate first, you need only look up. A poorly insulated attic lets rising hot air escape in the winter and searing air radiate downward in the summer. According to the DOE, your attic could be guilty of up to 40% of your home's energy loss. The good news is that most attics are easy to insulate. Chances are it won't take you more than a weekend to make this important energy upgrade.

In addition to upgrading your insulation, consider having an attic vent fan installed. It has a thermostat that turns the fan on when the attic heats up. Setting the thermostat at 85°F is typical. Because the vent fan is mounted in the roof or in a gable, you'll likely want to hire a pro for the job.

CHECK WHAT YOU HAVE. The type and depth of insulation in your attic is your guide to how much R-value you already have. In most attics, the floor, rather than the underside of the roof, is insulated. Measure the thickness of the insulation.

QUICK TIP If you have any doubt about what type insulation you have, snap a digital picture and get an opinion at your home center.

CALCULATING HOW MUCH INSULATION YOU NEED

Use the chart below to calculate the R-value (the resistance of a material to heat flow) of the insulation in your attic. For example, if you find you have 5½ in. of rock wool, multiply 5.5 times 2.8 for an R-value of 15.4. Then check your zone on p. 21 for how much additional insulation you should install.

WHAT YOU SEE		WHAT IT IS	R-VALUE CALCULATOR
Fiberglass batt	Yellow, pink, or white fibers, sometimes paper or foil backing	Fiberglass	Depth in inches x 3.2
Loose rock wool (blown in)	Small yellow, pink, white bits	Fiberglass	Depth in inches x 2.5
	Gray bits	Rock wool	Depth in inches x 2.8
	Flat gray newsprint pieces	Cellulose	Depth in inches x 3.7
Vermiculite granules	Small, spongy, mica-like pieces	Vermiculite or Perlite	Depth in inches x 2.7

How to Cut Insulation

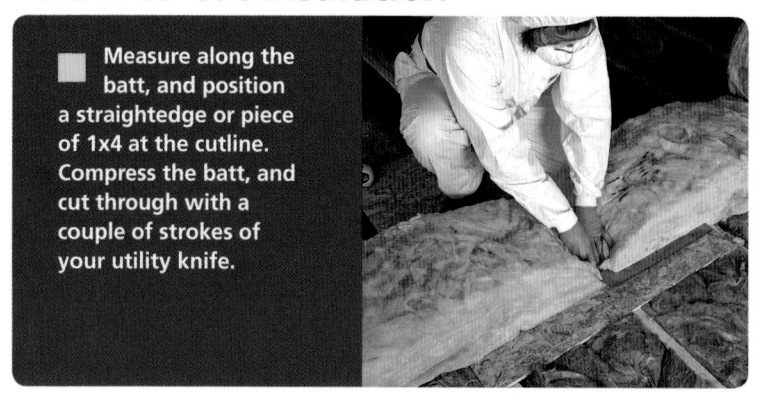

Measure along the batt, and position a straightedge or piece of 1x4 at the cutline. Compress the batt, and cut through with a couple of strokes of your utility knife.

LOCATION, LOCATION

The DOE recommends a range of R-30 to R-60 for attics. Use the map below to help determine exactly how much insulation you need to add. For example, if you live in Chicago (Zone 5), you need a minimum R-value of 38. If you already have 5½ in. of rock wool (R-value 15.4), you need to add about an R-value of 23. Adding an 8-in. to 8¼-in. R-25 batt comes closest, giving you a total R-value of 40.4.

ZONE 1	ZONE 2	ZONE 3	ZONE 4	ZONE 5	ZONES 6–8
R-30 to R-49	R-30 to R-60	R-30 to R-60	R-38 to R-60	R-38 to R-60	R-49 to R-60

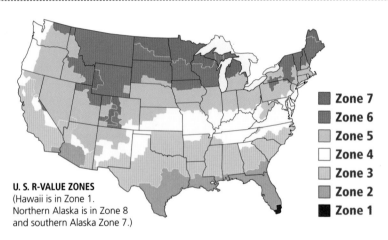

Zone 7
Zone 6
Zone 5
Zone 4
Zone 3
Zone 2
Zone 1

U. S. R-VALUE ZONES
(Hawaii is in Zone 1.
Northern Alaska is in Zone 8
and southern Alaska Zone 7.)

Fiberglass batt R-value	R-11	R-13	R-15	R-19	R-21	R-25	R-30	R-38
Thickness, standard	3½ in.	3⅝ in.	–	6 to 6¼ in.	–	8 to 8¼ in.	9½ in.	12 in.
Thickness, high density	–	–	3½ in.	–	5¼ in.	–	8 in.	–

CALCULATE HOW MUCH INSULATION YOU'LL NEED

Batt insulation is the most DIY-friendly insulation, and because it comes compressed in plastic bundles, it is easy to get up into your attic. Measure the width and length of your attic to determine the total square footage. Next, find out how much area is covered by a bundle of insulation with the R-value you want. For example, an R-19 bundle of standard batting covers just over 87 sq. ft. An attic with a total area of 1,320 sq. ft. would need just over 15 bundles (1,320 ÷ 87 = 15.17).

1. MEASURE BETWEEN THE JOISTS. Ceiling joists are typically 16 in. or 24 in. on center. Measure between the joists to determine the width of batts you'll need— 15 in. or 23 in.

2. MEASURE THE LENGTH AND WIDTH OF THE ATTIC. Use a tape measure to find the length and width or your attic. Multiply the length and width for the total square footage.

PREPPING FOR ATTIC INSULATION

You are entering itch country, so wear long sleeves, safety goggles, mask, and gloves. Knee pads can be handy too—you'll be kneeling most of the time. Get a 3-ft. by 4-ft. piece of ½-in. plywood or oriented strand board (OSB) to use as a work platform. When moving about, be sure to step only on joists.

What You'll Need: Insulation; vent baffles; tape measure; utility knife; straightedge; stapler

1. SET UP A WORK PLATFORM. To
avoid stepping between the joists and cracking through the ceiling below, set up your work platform.

 QUICK TIP For maximum protection, buy a disposable painting coverall. For less than $15, you get seamless protection—a hood and elastic at the wrists and ankles.

2. INSTALL EAVES VENT BAFFLES.
Rigid-foam vent baffles help air circulate up from the eaves vent to push moist air out of ridge or gable vents. Check between rafters for an eaves vent. You'll see some daylight or feel the flow of air where there is a vent. Don't expect to find one between every pair of rafters. Where you find one, pull back the insulation and staple the baffle in place.

STANLEY

ADD THE INSULATION

Now the fun starts. With all the prep done, you'll cover a lot of ground quickly. To avoid tracking fiberglass throughout the house, have an assistant or two push the wrapped bundles into the attic.

1. NOTCH AROUND THE RAFTERS.
Where the batts run parallel to the attic wall, use a utility knife to notch for rafters.

2. STAGGER THE JOINTS. Roll out the batts so they butt over a joist to make sure you are not leaving a gap in your coverage. As extra protection, stagger the joints.

Insulating Can Lights

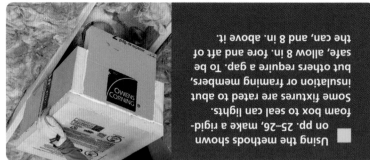

■ Using the methods shown on pp. 25–26, make a rigid-foam box to seal can lights. Some fixtures are rated to abut insulation or framing members, but others require a gap. To be safe, allow 8 in. fore and aft of the can, and 8 in. above it.

MAKING A RIGID-FOAM BOX

An attic hatchway is a prime culprit for energy loss. Measure to be sure your completed box overlaps the opening. Make sure that when completed it will fit through the hatchway and into the attic. A circular saw makes quick work of rigid foam. The box shown is 32 in. wide, 68 in. long, and 10 in. high—more than large enough for the typical attic ladder.

What You'll Need: 4x8 2-in. sheet of rigid-foam insulation; adhesive caulk; tape measure; framing square; circular saw; caulk gun; tape; 3 ft. of 1x2; spring clamps

1. CUT THE RIGID FOAM. Lay two 2x2s or 2x4s on sawhorses to support the rigid foam as it is cut. Using a circular saw, cut the sides for the box.

2. ASSEMBLE RIGID-FOAM SIDES.
With an adhesive rated for rigid foam, glue the pieces together. Using a framing square to square up the corners, tape the joints to hold them until the adhesive dries.

▶

STANLEY

3. CUT AND GLUE HANDLES.
Using a miter box and fine-toothed saw, cut one 10-in. and two 3-in. pieces of 1x2 for each handle you need. Glue and clamp them as shown.

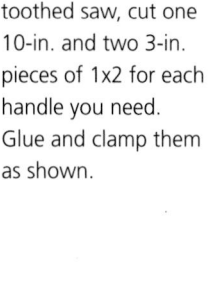

4. CUT AND ASSEMBLE THE LID.
Measure the box, and cut a lid to sit on top of it. Use foam scraps as spacers on the ends so the lid sits squarely in the box. Adhering a handle to the top and bottom makes the lid easy to handle.

5. INSTALL THE BOX.
Position the box over your stairs, and fasten it to the floor using adhesive around the perimeter and 2x2 strips at each end. Check the fit of the lid.

INSULATE DUCTWORK

A forced-air heating, ventilation, and air-conditioning (HVAC) system circulates heated or cooled air through sheet-metal ducts. Often these ducts pass through an unconditioned area of the house like a basement, crawlspace, or attic. Save energy by insulating the ducts where you can get to them.

What You'll Need: Plastic foil insulation; foil tape; scissors

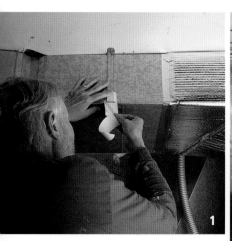

1. WRAP EXPOSED DUCTS. Use small strips of foil tape to seal any holes or loose joints in the ductwork. Cut the amount of foil roll insulation you need. Using foil tape, attach it to the duct.

 QUICK TIP Where a duct runs between joists, cover it with a strip of rigid-foam insulation.

2. SEAL WITH FOIL TAPE. As you work along the duct, overlap the insulation slightly before taping the seams.

INSTALL A PROGRAMMABLE THERMOSTAT

A programmable thermostat lets you be frugal with energy by choosing the setting and timing in advance and then not have to fuss with it—or be tempted to cheat on your energy-conservation measures. Before starting this project, switch off the breaker to the HVAC system (see p. 16). As you work, bend or clip the wires so they don't fall into the wall.

What You'll Need: New thermostat; small slot or Phillips screwdriver; wire stripper; drill/driver and bits

1. REMOVE THE OLD THERMOSTAT. Pry off the cover of your thermostat. Check that the color coding of the wires is correct—white wire to white terminal, red wire to red terminal, etc. If there is any doubt, label the wire. Remove the thermostat.

2. INSTALL THE WALL PLATE. Carefully feed the wires into the new wall plate. Level it while marking for the wall anchors and install them. Attach and level the wall plate.

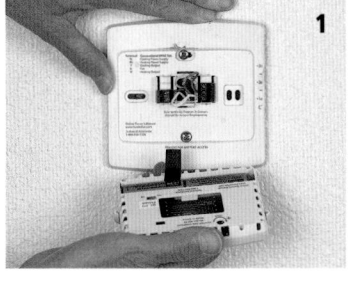

> **QUICK TIP** Change your fiberglass furnace filters once a month in season. Or, buy pleated filters that only need to be changed every three months or so.

3. CONNECT THE WIRES. Trim, strip, and connect the wires to the new thermostat. Clip the unit in place, restore power, and program the thermostat.

TURN DOWN THE WATER HEATER

Most water heaters come from the factory set at 140°F. However, most households do fine with 120°F water. Cranking down the thermostat 20°F saves you 6% to 10% in energy costs

QUICK TIP If your heater feels warm to the touch or doesn't have an R-24 rating or greater, add a water-heater blanket. According to the DOE, it can cut heat loss by as much as 45%, reducing your energy bill by 4% to 9%.

2. CHECK THE WATER TEMPERATURE. Use a meat thermometer to check the temperature at the hot-water faucet farthest from the heater. Wait two hours and check the temperature again. Once you get the temperature you want, mark the thermostat for future reference.

1. ADJUST THE THERMOSTAT. Reset the thermostat, estimating the needed reduction. Some thermostats do not have temperature markings; when they do, they are often inaccurate.

QUICK TIP Drain your water heater every year to remove energy-stealing sediment.

TAME YOUR APPLIANCES

Small changes of habit can yield noticeable energy savings. For example, using ice cube trays instead of an automatic ice maker cuts a refrigerator's energy use by 14% to 20%, according to the DOE's EnergyStar. And your fridge may be set colder than needed. Aim for 37°F to 40°F in the fridge and 0°F to 5°F in the freezer. Run only full loads through your dishwasher. Except for cakes and bread, preheating the oven is seldom necessary.

2. SIZE THE PAN TO THE BURNER. A pan should cover the burner or element. With electric stoves, turn the element off a minute or two early. Residual heat keeps things bubbling.

1. CLEAN FRIDGE COILS. Dusty condenser coils underneath or behind your refrigerator make it harder for the fridge to vent heat. Vacuum the coils every few months. If the coils are on the back of the fridge, position the appliance 3 in. from the wall to aid circulation.

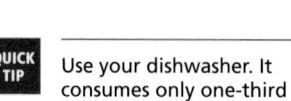

QUICK TIP Use your dishwasher. It consumes only one-third of the water needed for hand-washing dishes. If you have the option, skip the energy-intensive dry cycle.

CHOOSING ENERGY-EFFICIENT LIGHT BULBS

Lighting eats up about 12% of the energy used in a typical house. By simply replacing incandescent bulbs with energy-saving compact fluorescent lamps (CFLs) or light-emitting diode (LED) bulbs, you cut your lighting costs substantially. Both require lower wattage for the same light. For example, to replace a 60-watt incandescent bulb, you need only a 15-watt CFL or a 12-watt LED.

COMPACT FLUORESCENT LAMP. CFLs save up to 75% in energy. The moon-glow light quality and slight buzzing are things of the past. New bulbs cast a warm, silent light and last up to 9 years. On the downside, they take awhile to fully warm up. Not all are suitable for outdoor use: Check the rating. A CFL contains a small amount of mercury, a danger if broken and warranting careful disposal.

LIGHT-EMITTING DIODE. The slightly more expensive LED bulbs save up to 80% in energy and last 20 years or more. LEDs light up quickly and emit so little heat you can touch them. The downside: Color characteristics vary between brands and can change with age.

QUICK TIP Position lamps in a corner. The walls reflect light, allowing you to use a lower-wattage bulb.

INSTALLING AN OCCUPANCY SENSOR

An occupancy sensor automatically switches lights on when you enter a room. If it senses no motion for a period of time, it switches the lights off. It's an ideal solution for basements, garages, and other areas where it's hard to notice that a light has been left on. Occupancy sensors are rated for a single switch (single pole) as shown here, or for two switches (three-way). Switch off the power at the breaker panel (see p. 16).

1. DETACH THE SWITCH. Remove the switch plate and unfasten the switch from the box. Pull the switch out and test to confirm the power is off. Disconnect the wires.

2. MAKE THE CONNECTIONS. Connect the green ground wire and bare silver wire to the bare copper wire. Connect the other wires. Typically, the two black leads connect to two black wires in the box. Sometimes one is black and the other is a white wire marked with a black marker. Hold the stripped ends side-by-side, and twist on the wire nuts.

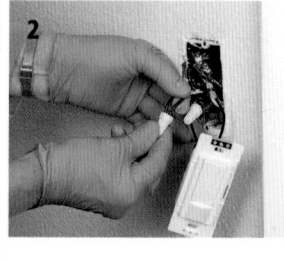

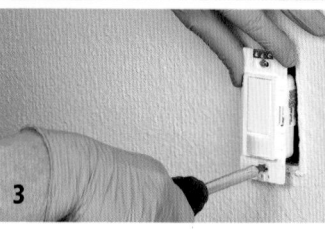

3. INSTALL THE SENSOR AND PROGRAM. Carefully fold the wires in the box, and fasten the sensor and switch plate. Most sensors are preset to turn off the fixture after 5 minutes. The type shown has 1-, 5-, 15-, and 30-minute options. Simply hold the button down, wait for the lens to signal the setting you want, and then release.